Soror Kerri,
It's time to go to the next level.
#letsgrow

It's Growth Time!

6 Intentional Growth Strategies That Will Set You Up For Greatness

Kimberly Burke

ISBN: 978-0-9864290-2-6
Digital ISBN: 978-0-9864290-3-3
Library of Congress Control Number: 2016921135

Edited and formatted by: Farabee Publishing
www.farabeepublishing.com

Book cover design by: Uncommon Chick Media
www.uncommonchickmedia.com

Author photography by: Cory Lampkin
www.corylampkinproductions.com

Also available as an eBook on Amazon Kindle.

To order additional copies of this book, contact the author:
Kimberly Burke at info@coachkimburke.com
Website: www.coachkimburke.com

Printed in the United States of America.

QKE4GROWTH
Inspiring people to achieve their personal goals

DEDICATION

This book is dedicated to my sister, Kassie Burke. Your perseverance and your drive inspires me. You have always been there for me and encouraged me when I could not encourage myself. You've seen my struggle and you've heard my cries. Our bond is divine. Kassie it is time for you to grow to your full potential. It is time that you put yourself first. I love you and I am here to help you grow.

#ItsGrowthTime

"Growth is painful. Change is painful. But nothing is as painful as staying stuck somewhere you don't belong."

~ Unknown ~

CONTENTS

INTRODUCTION

"Everyone thinks of changing the world,

but no one thinks of changing himself."

~ Leo Tolstoy ~

Slap Yourself

I was finishing up one of my greatest speeches and people were clapping all around me. I was a guest speaker at one of my sisters in business, Coach Sierra Rainge, premier event called 'Discover Your Beauty Brunch,' in Phoenix, Arizona.

I was excited and I could feel that my words moved the audience and someone was ready to grow. Suddenly there was a question on the floor. It wasn't that I was unprepared for questions, but I was caught up in the excitement of nailing my speech and seeing the impression of enjoyment on people faces. The lady asked, "What happens when you don't achieve your goals?" My mouth opened, and words came out before I could think. I said, "You should slap yourself!"

Uh-Oh! Did I just tell people to slap themselves if they did not achieve their goals? You are damn right!

It is time for you to get out of your own damn way. You have been holding yourself back for years, months, weeks, and countless days. The time is now for you to achieve the things you have always wanted. The time is now for you to be great. The time is now for you to become an Unapologetic Goal Getter.

Who cares? I care. I care about your well-being. I care you are hurting because of your past experiences with heartbreak, career let downs, family/spouse disapproval, and negative self-talk with your inner being.

It's killing you softly that you work 40 hours or more a week to achieve company goals with little to no appreciation of the work you do. I get it because that use to be my thinking. I also get that you have bills to pay, well so do I.

Keeping my sanity and achieving my goals was more of a priority than doing something that was suffocating me from my greatness.

Working for a company that undervalues you is not worth the stress and the mental abuse. Getting a paycheck on the 15th and the 30th is not merely enough. You should set yourself up for greatness by having other streams of income.

You can start now. *Yes, while you keep your good job.* You can start to become clearer about what you want to do next. It can be starting a business, creating a product/service for the community, or even change careers so you can work with a company that values you.

Stop playing the victim, you are greater than that. You deserve better and you must do better. Playing the blame game is not for Queens. We own up to our fears and we make things happen, no matter what.

Slap yourself!

Get over it and ***#LetsGrow***

This is your Wake Up call.

"The positive thinker sees the invisible, feels the intangible, and achieves the impossible."

~ Anonymous ~

6 Personal Growth Strategies That Work

I felt propelled to write this book because there is someone out there who has given up on their dreams.

The things they always wanted to accomplish in life are memories because they did not possess the "I Will Spirit". It's not I can, but it's I will become a doctor one day, a best-selling author, a transformational speaker, and a woman of influence in the community. You have to want your goals bad enough you dare yourself to achieve them. Having the "I Will Spirit" places you in the position to WIN by your own rules.

The 6 Personal Growth Strategies That Work is just for you. These strategies will help you become refocused on your goals and achieve them with intention.

I define a Personal Growth Strategy (PGS) as *a plan of action to maximize self-improvement to achieve personal goals*. If you do not have a plan, how can you achieve your desired results effectively?

Great satisfaction overcomes you when you reach and achieve your goal. This feeling makes you want to keep setting goals and achieving them all the time.

The word intention is often overlooked. It's one of the most important ways you can achieve your personal goals. That's why you should live a life of intention.

According to the Merriam-Webster dictionary, *intention is the thing that you plan to do or achieve; an aim or purpose.*

To be great, you must intentionally do things every day that will get you closer to your goal. Being more intentional in your approach can jumpstart positive results.

The Personal Growth Strategy Cycle

1) **Divine Intervention:** You Must Seek a Higher Power to Find Your Purpose

2) **Write It Down:** You Have To See Your Goals Daily

3) **Research, and Research Again:** You Must Follow Systems That Work

4) **Build Relationships:** You Have To Develop Great Relationships

5) **Do Your Growth Work:** You Must Execute Your Personal Growth Plan

6) **Reward & Praise:** You Have To Acknowledge Your Greatness and Give Praise Where It's Due

The Growth Experience

Growth Analysis:

Before you start to read about the 6 Personal Growth Strategies That Work, take this survey to get an analysis of where you are right now on your growth journey.

To move forward you must know where you are and where you came from.

Directions: Read each statement and circle Yes or No to answer.

1	I look in the mirror at least three times a day because I enjoy looking at myself.	Yes	No
2	I am a starter, but I have a hard time finishing things in life.	Yes	No
3	I have a personal growth plan for the next 10 years of my life.	Yes	No
4	I like working alone because no one can help me get to the next level.	Yes	No
5	I am still holding a grudge against someone who hurt me more than a year ago.	Yes	No
6	I am ready to take my life to the next level, no matter what.	Yes	No
7	I struggle with self-confidence.	Yes	No
8	I am free to do whatever makes me happy.	Yes	No
9	I volunteer with community projects because I love helping others.	Yes	No
10	I am not afraid to talk about my purpose, my passion, or my story.	Yes	No

What Does This Data Mean?

If you are anything like me, you probably want to know what this data means. Did you have more Yes' circled or No's.

The truth is that is doesn't matter how many Yes' or No's you received. I want you to get past receiving the right answer. I want you create a deeper understanding around **'WHY'** you answered in the way you did. Re-read each question and look at your results.

To set yourself up for greatness, you have to learn the importance of self-reflection. Real growth is when you start checking yourself. I have to check myself on a regular basis. Do I like it? Nope!

You will not like it either. My imperfections allow me to be vulnerable with my Goal Getter clients.

They can see me grow along with them. I provide all I know and then recommend other services when I have identified that they need an entire team working with them to achieve their goal.

Use the space below to write out why you responded the way you did to each statement on the survey.

How did your results make you feel? Are you upset that you don't know whether having more Yes' or No's determine if you are ideal for success?

Why or why not? This is your time to be honest with yourself about your growth process.

Growth Analysis Reflection

How To Use This Book

This book is designed to be a new wave of growth for you. It is enriched with so many tools to encourage you to set yourself up for greatness. This book is for people who will practice self-discipline to achieve their goals. It will help you grow from the inside out.

I believe self-reflection is the turning point for you to grow to the next level. If you cannot be self-reflective then you will continue to blame others for your shortcomings and it could be the reason you are not achieving your goals.

Throughout these chapters, you'll find some growth quotes to keep you inspired about setting your goals and why it's important to stay focused. These quotes will help you remember that you are not alone on this journey and that others have reached their goals, and so can you.

At the end of each chapter you'll find the Growth Journey and Execution List sections. The Growth Journey section provides you journaling space to self-reflect on things you want to remember along your path to greatness.

The Execution List section provides a blank chart for you to write specific tasks down that you need to complete after reading the chapter. This exercise is vital for you to keep up with things that must be completed along your journey.

Take the time to reflect after each chapter to honestly be at one with yourself. They say that you can fool others, but you can't fool yourself.

Don't rob yourself from the truth that lies within you. Get in formation and start the next steps to intentionally achieve your goals.

Growth Quotes: Inspirational quotes to keep you excited to achieve your goals while reading.

Growth Journey: This is where you will begin some self-reflection. Summarize the main points from the chapter that will help you along your growth journey. You can also write down your favorite page numbers that you want to refer to or tell a friend about.

Execution List: This is your time to write out your tasks that you need to make to achieve your goal after readying the chapters. Think about the steps you need to take to execute like a Goal Getter. Be realistic when writing out your tasks.

"I didn't know if anyone would care to listen to my message, but I knew with all my heart that if I could just touch the life of one person through my work then it would all be worth it."

~ Joe Duncan ~

Abandonment to Encouragement

I never knew if I was going to witness death at any moment in my mother's household. Living with my mother and her new husband was like living on a battlefield. I felt like I was a little solider fighting a hopeless war between two people who would die killing each other before leaving each other.

I went to bed each night praying that the noise will end. The noise was as loud as someone blasting their trap music in a car. I could not sleep because behind closed doors the sound of drunkenness involved fists to fists, rude conduct, drug and alcohol manipulation, the rivalry of love, and so much more.

I experienced years of trauma witnessing domestic violence. I walked on egg shells for years not knowing when something was going to pop off. It was painful and no matter how much I begged my mother to leave her abusive husband, she wouldn't.

I was only 16 when I felt a fast blast of hopelessness. I was considering giving up and allowing the chips to fall where they may. When my mother told me and my older sister we had to get out of her house, I knew something was psychologically wrong with her.

I couldn't believe, what I perceived to be an altercation of her drunkenness, was indeed reality. She had chosen her abusive and drunken husband over her two beautiful daughters.

She chose him over my older sister and I. For that I have been ashamed of my story of abandonment from my mother for years.

Seeing domestic violence first hand for countless years is traumatizing. Per statistics from Children of Domestic Violence: kids from a domestic violence household are 3 times more likely to repeat the cycle in adulthood.

They are also 6 times more likely to commit suicide and 50 times more likely to abuse drugs. The most alarming statistic, I read, from the Children of Domestic Violence website, was that children who have experienced domestic violence often meet the criteria for Post-Traumatic Stress Disorder (PTSD) and the effects on their brain are like those of combat war veterans.

I spent many nights journaling my thoughts and praying that God will break this historical curse of domestic violence, insecurity, and hopelessness.

I am thankful that those facts did not consume me. I am not a statistic to those previous facts. However, I did experience constant battles with myself.

Throughout my teenage years and early adulthood, I would suffocate myself from being all that I could be. Even though I was good at some things, often I felt unworthy. I fought my insecurities, my bitterness, my need to be right, my physical appearance, and any other inner conflict.

I had been at war with me for so long I had lost sight of who I was. I questioned God about my situation as a teenager and even asked him: Why am I here? What is required of me? Why am I hopeless?

God Is Still In The Saving Business

My village answered my prayers. I received an outpouring of love from family members, non-family members, and even women whom I call my Godmothers who took me in under their wings.

I lived from house to house with no consistency and it was at that time I knew I had to create a plan for my next steps.

In the word of God it says, *"For a brief moment I abandoned you, but with deep compassion I will bring you back."* (Isiah 54:7, NIV)

As a believer, I know God had allowed the separation from my mother to happen to protect me. Had I not gone through being put out of my mother's house, without having a plan, who would have known what my goal achievement strategies would look like.

Who would have known I could execute effectively: my plan of going to college, getting a good job, and moving away from my hometown? However, I was still struggling with inner conflicts.

I had to intentionally listen to gospel music to encourage myself. It was songs by Bishops Paul S. Morton, Marvin Sapp, Yolanda Adams, and The Clarke Sisters that kept me going.

I can be rest assured that now when I hear Marvin Sapp sing his song 'My Testimony,' I can sing boldly, *I got some scars, but I'm still alive, In spite of calamity, He still has a plan for me and it's working out for my good, and it's building my testimony.*

When The Clarke Sisters sing, 'Blessed and Highly Favored,' I get chills in my body because I know *It could have been me, it should have been me, it would have been me, if it wasn't for the blood…* I can stand today and say that the struggle was real, but so were my blessings.

Forgive and You Will Be Set Free

In order to be restored from my personal self-sabotage I had to dig deeper than I ever had before. I had to learn how to forgive my mother and even my biological father for allowing me to stay with her.

Forgiveness blocks blessings, so I had to learn how to forgive my parents and other people in my life from apologies I never got. It was hard for me, but not hard for God. I had to forgive them so that I could live peacefully and really move on with my life.

Forgiveness was the solid key for me and it opened doors to my mental psyche that I had never had before.

What's Your Plan?

During my pain, I found happiness in serving others. It was in the serving of others where I ultimately found myself.

I later found out in young adulthood I needed to be the person I never received when I was younger. I needed to be more responsible, more confident, more positive, and more intentional. I needed a growth plan to prepare for my journey, so I created one.

My personal growth plan included my innovative goal setting cycle that I talk about in my book called *The Code to Greatness*.

Clarity

Options

Discipline

Execution

Creating a plan and working my plan saved my life for further occurrences in not being ready. Now, I stay ready for whatever comes my way. I accept stumbling blocks because it's all a part of God's plan.

I didn't forget where I came from, I just woke up and realized that I could not stay there. It was time for me to make some changes.

It was time for me to inspire others with my story. It was time for me to grow intentionally. Getting out of my own way and refilling my thoughts with positivity was what I needed to achieve my personal goals.

I had to recognize that the conflicts I had with myself was only preventing me from setting myself up for greatness. Most people have inner conflicts too. I am a living proof that self-doubt and fear can ruin your self-confidence until you stand up against it. Call it by name and decide that you are ready to get out of your own way.

"I survived because the fire inside me burned brighter than the fire around me."

~Joshua Graham~

Chapter 2 Growth Journey

Summarize the main points from this chapter that will help you along your growth journey.

SELF-REFLECTION

Chapter 2 Execution List

Make a list of tasks that you need to complete to achieve your goal after reading this chapter.

TASK LIST	COMPLETION DATE
1.	
2.	
3.	
4.	
5.	
6.	
7.	
8.	
9.	
10.	

"If you don't know where you are going, every road will lead you nowhere."

~ Anonymous ~

1ST Growth Strategy - Divine Intervention

Growing up in a Baptist church I am reminded of a song we use to sing, *Just A Little Talk with Jesus.* In this song, there is a verse that says, *"I may have doubts and fears my eyes be filled with tears, but Jesus is a friend who watches day and night, I go to him in prayer he knows my every care, and just a little talk with my Jesus makes it right."*

I want you to try again, but this time with God. I believe in the Father, the Son, and the Holy Spirit. You may have a different belief system and that's ok. I am not here to convert you, but I am here to encourage you that before you set your goals, pray and ask a higher power to lead you.

This may take some time and you will need to listen to receive that which is destined for you. Simply ask God these two questions, what am I called to do? Who am I called to serve? You may not get an answer right away, but I want you to keep the faith. I want you to respect the process. It may take a while. When it hits your spirit, you will know.

I recall having an epiphany in January 2013 to start a business with a mission to help others, but it wasn't until March 2014 that my business, Queen Kim Enterprises, LLC dba QKE 4 Growth, came into fruition. I thought I was ready in 2013, but God had other plans for my life. It took time, prayer, and much preparation. Once I started my business, doors began to open and it could not have been a better time. Everything was done decent and in order because of God's timing.

What is Divine Intervention?

I believe there is a divine way of doing things. I call it a Divine Path: Divine Order + Divine Connections = Divine Intervention. When you do things in order combined with divine connections from the Holy Spirit, you will experience divine intervention.

When things are out of order it causes confusion. There cannot be any order in mess. When things often become too messy in my life, I have seen God disrupt everything. I call them divine disruptions. Having a plan is essential, but sometimes God challenges our plan. Allow your plan to be guided by God. Pray before you set one and be prayerful throughout the process. I have noticed when people do their own thing (myself included) God gives them more divine disruptions to put them back on the right path.

"If you can get the inside right, the outside will fall into place."

~Eckhart Tolle~

Why Do You Want It So Bad?

Creating a WHY statement is vital when you want to achieve your goals. When your WHY is clear, the how is easy as you grow along your journey. I challenge my Goal Getters to create WHY statements in their very first session with me. This allows them to set a reason for why attaining their goals is important. It gives them an affirmation statement to believe in. Do you know why you want to achieve your goals?

Make sure the goals you set are for you and not to please others. You should want to reach your goals because you have a desire for them. They should be goals you cannot see yourself leaving this earth without completing. Your goals should be high enough for you to reach them. They are your goals and others may not understand why and that's ok.

"But God" Testimony

In my heart, I always keep a "But God" testimony. A "But God" testimony is when you know you were on the verge of giving up, when you thought you could not make it.

When you have given your all and it looked like all your resources were depleted, but God stepped in and made everything work out in your favor. Have you ever had a But God testimony?

I recall having to take a state English test in the education field. I had taken the test the first time with little to no studying – I failed.

I felt horrible. So, I took a pre-assessment to prepare for my next test – I still failed. I was angry. Why could I not pass this test?

This time I not only reviewed my pre-assessment, I was tutored from two different people. I failed again, this time only 3 points away from passing.

Now, I was really upset. What on earth was I doing wrong? This time I not only studied and met with tutors, I started to question God.

I asked him how I could be a woman with two high level degrees (B.S. and a M.A.) not pass a simple state English test. I felt like he was not answering me.

The day I was going to take the test for the fourth time, I recall being in my car driving along the highway headed to the testing center. I was praying and fussing with God.

I told him in your word (The Bible) you said this, you said that, and why aren't you doing any of it. You know, how we can get…. Am I the only one who questions God?

I pulled into the testing center. The people knew my face. I was now a regular. I was embarrassed and my self-esteem level had decreased.

Here I was again taking a simple state English test. I did everything the same. I went to the questions I knew first, skipped the ones I seconded guess on, etc. I was effectively using my testing strategies. I finished the test.

I didn't want to leave the room and check-out. I had taken the test so much, I just didn't have any hope.

I went to the lady at check-out. She had a blank look on her face. Normally she shakes her head no when I come out with a sad face. This time I could not read her face. She handed me my testing completion paper.

I PASSED. Oh, my God! I started jumping up and down praising God right in that testing center. What on earth did I do differently? I tried several times before to pass this simple state English test on my own. The only difference that stood out is that I had a no-nonsense conversation with God.

The one who is all knowing. The one who needed me to confess that I needed him. I passed because this time I tried with God.

My favorite scripture: *"If ye shall ask anything in my name, I will do it."* (John 14:14 KJV).

Deliver Me from Me

You want growth, but you are not comfortable in your own skin. You have not embraced who you are now, so how can you be ready for who you are about to become?

Understanding your present moment is essential to move to the next moment in your life. You can have the intent to move forward, but your present moment is bad and you cannot seem to think about your 'next'.

What is the inner conversation going on within you? The worst place you can be under attack is in your own head. Negative self-talk can destroy your inner being. It is the most powerful form of communication.

You must intentionally control what goes on in your mind. It can either help you or hurt you. Remember in Chapter 2 when I shared my story about how I allowed internal oppression to steal my worthiness.

Don't let that happen to you. Learn from my mistakes and change the negative conversations you have with yourself to be positive ones.

To do this, you will need to begin to program your thoughts to love you and inspire you to go after the things that you desire.

This can be difficult to do, especially if you have been dealing with negative self-talk for years. You can overcome negative self-talk by:

- Praying specifically to release negative thoughts.
- Listening to positive messages.
- Reading self-help books that inspire you to be greater.
- Counting your blessings.
- Telling your inner voice to Shut Up!

You must train your mind. Les Brown stated that negative thoughts are like weeds. They grow through the cracks in sidewalks.

So, you could be a strong person, but even strong people must continue to place positivity in their lives. Remember, what you think about, you bring about.

You have the power to control your thoughts. Decide on who you want to be and get out of your own damn way.

Repeat this:

Fear does not live here.

Fear does not live here.

Fear does not live here anymore!

Chapter 3 Growth Journey

Summarize the main points from this chapter that will help you along your growth journey.

SELF-REFLECTION

Chapter 3 Execution List

Make a list of tasks that you need to complete to achieve your goal after reading this chapter.

TASK LIST	COMPLETION DATE
1.	
2.	
3.	
4.	
5.	
6.	
7.	
8.	
9.	
10.	

"The first step towards getting somewhere is to decide that you are not going to stay

where you are."

~ Unknown ~

2ND Growth Strategy - Write It Down

John Rohn said it best,

> "It's challenging to be a student of your own life, your own future, and your own destiny. Don't trust your memory. When you listen to something valuable, write it down. When you come across something important, write it down. Take the time to keep notes and keep a journal."

Where do you keep your goals? Are they in your journal? Are they on a poster? Where do you keep all your magnificent thoughts?

Your answer to these questions will determine if you are just talking about your goals or are you are serious about reaching your goals. People who write down their goals are closer to goal achievement than the people who don't.

Writing in the Dark

Have you ever thought of something and forgot to write it down? Well, that has been me time after time. Now, I keep journals and notepads in my purse, car, desk, tables at home, and especially on my nightstand. You are probably wondering why I would keep a notepad on my nightstand.

At night when I am sleeping and I receive a word, I turn over and start writing what has been revealed to me. I know this may sound crazy, but I am writing in the dark.

I do not turn on a light to wake my husband, I do not keep a mini flashlight on my nightstand, I just simply write.

When I awake, my handwriting may be hard to read, but it is worth it. I do not waste time. When God drops words in my spirit, I must write it down immediately. I want you to intentionally start keeping a handy dandy notebook always to write down your thoughts.

In the event a notebook is forgotten, be like me and write them down on receipts, church programs, flyers, napkins, etc. Don't wait until later to jot down your thoughts because you may forget it.

Do it while you think about it so you can intentionally do what's needed to prepare you for what will come next.

I am not a product of my circumstances. I am a product of my decisions.

~ Stephen Covey ~

I recommend you start journaling daily. Journaling is one of my greatest stress relievers. Whenever I am feeling down, I write. Whenever I am feeling good, I write. I just love to write.

It is my outlet. I would rather write my thoughts down than to allow my thoughts to consume me. I don't know about you, but too much goes on in this big head of mine.

You should not only write down your goals, but you should hang them up so that you can see them every day.

I have a wall full of my recent accomplishments and vision boards. I can see how much I have grown over the years and see how much more I can intentionally accomplish my goals by looking at my vision boards daily.

Do you see the pattern? I see my goals daily. Writing them down is great, but you need to see it and believe that you can achieve it.

Chapter 4 Growth Journey

Summarize the main points from this chapter that will help you along your growth journey

SELF-REFLECTION

Chapter 4 Execution List

Make a list of tasks that you need to complete to achieve your goal after reading this chapter.

TASK LIST	COMPLETION DATE
1.	
2.	
3.	
4.	
5.	
6.	
7.	
8.	
9.	
10.	

"We are only blind as we want to be."

~ Dr. Maya Angelou ~

3RD Growth Strategy – Research and Research Again

Research never ends. Research starts in the beginning of your growth journey and continually grows throughout the goal achievement process.

In undergrad I had no desire to research in Psychological Statistics. I would dread going to the library and spending countless hours on finding the right paper that supports whatever we may have been focused on.

It was just not what I enjoyed doing. However, the more practice, the better I became at researching psychological databases. Researching in undergrad has been by far the most intuitive research I have every achieved.

By researching you will find the most effective resources you will need to reach your goals. People love to say, "I didn't see it, I couldn't find it, etc." You did not look hard enough.

We live in the 21st century where information is at our fingertips. You can google anything and it pops up. You can watch YouTube videos from the comfort of your own home and duplicate things, as you see fit.

Our ancestors had little to no resources and they achieved their goals beyond our imagination. They applied this research, and strategy to intentionally achieve their goals.

This is not rocket science. You must be willing to research the market and know what's out there. It can be as simple as finding out what other people did successfully to achieve their goal. You are searching for the answers of what they did to accomplish their goals.

You do not have to make the same mistakes as others. There are proven strategies in the world that work. Ask yourself these questions?

What do I need to focus on first for my research efforts?

____

____

____

How will researching this topic help me achieve my goals?

____

____

____

Who has excelled at doing what I want to do? How can I learn from them?

____

____

____

The Fear of Success

You must forget about all the reasons your goal will not work for you and start thinking about the strategies that WILL work for you.

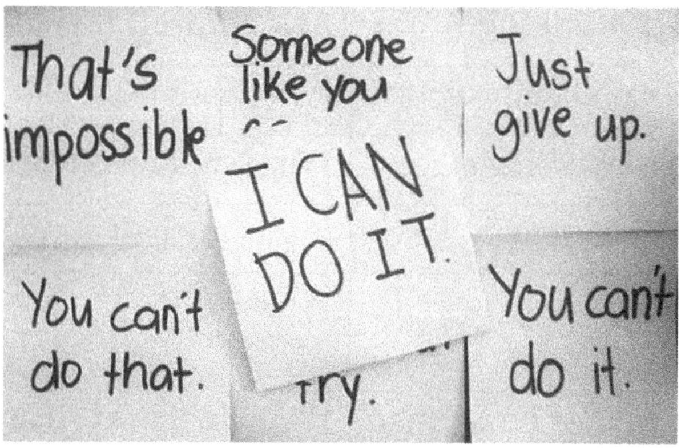

Don't give up on yourself before your journey has begun. Great things never came from comfort zones.

Don't be afraid of your own success. There is not enough room in your mind to allow both fear and faith to live there.

You must decide to keep faith or fear. Which one will you choose?

What Are You Thinking?

Don't give up on this research, and research again strategy. Research takes time. When you start seeing what others are doing, I want you to stay positive.

The objective is not for you to be like them, it's for you to see what they are doing. How can you fill a gap they may have overlooked? How can you market to your ideal client? How can you collaborate with others? How can you make a difference in the world?

Instead of thinking...	**Ask yourself this question...**
I am not good at this.	What are my strengths?
I made a mistake.	What am I missing?
This is good enough.	Is this my best work?
I give up!	What other strategies can I use?
I will never be better than him/her.	What do they do that works so well?
This is too hard.	How bad do I want it?
My plan didn't work.	What's my next step?

It's ok to make mistakes, but you must learn from them. Don't try to be a perfectionist. Trust me, I tried and it does not work. Faking perfections will set you up for failure. Be bold and make things happen for yourself. Just do it afraid.

"Lose the excuses. They don't get you any closer to your goals."

~ Angela Mader ~

Invest In Yourself

You need to start investing in yourself. Your research may show you need certain certifications, another degree, or more education from a special program.

You may have to attend live events outside your city. This will cost you. I did not promise that your research process would not incur a cost. How much are you willing to pay to get to the next level?

Now, I am not saying go take out a loan and become a slave to debt. No, No, No, No, No. Do not do that. What I am proposing to you is that you may have to pay the cost to be the boss.

Find out how much it is going to cost you to achieve your goals. Maybe the cost is free. I knew for me to start my own business, I had to pay an upfront cost of $50 to the State of Missouri for my LLC. That was it.

All the others things in starting my business came after that. You may not be starting a business, but whatever you are about to do count the costs beforehand.

That's why research, and research again is one of my growth strategies. Intentionally set yourself up for greatness financially.

Chapter 5 Growth Journey

Summarize the main points from this chapter that will help you along your growth journey.

SELF-REFLECTION

Chapter 5 Execution List

Make a list of tasks that you need to complete to achieve your goal after reading this chapter.

TASK LIST	COMPLETION DATE
1.	
2.	
3.	
4.	
5.	
6.	
7.	
8.	
9.	
10.	

"Don't chase people. Be yourself, do your own thing, and work hard. The right people – the ones who really belong in your life – will come to you and stay."

~ Will Smith ~

4TH Growth Strategy - Build Relationships

Look in the mirror. Stare at the image you see. Observe all the features of this person. The person staring back at you is your only competition. Anyone outside of this mirror is merely a way for you to cooperate and make a difference in the world.

As your life changes, so will your relationships. You must foster relationships with others. It's one thing to meet someone, but it's another thing to truly connect with them. There must be a social exchange opportunity and the value is relationship currency.

Wow! Imagine how wealthy you could be in cultivating relationships with people who can assist you along your growth journey and beyond. Everyone will not understand you, but the people that will, are going to connect with you at a high level.

I facilitated a growth workshop, *'Build Your Network to Build Your Net Worth,'* where people learn the importance of connecting with the right people. You must learn from a village of diverse people. I call them accountability partners.

Your accountability partners will most likely not be your best friend or a family member. I have found the best accountability partners in people who believe in my vision and who also achieving their own goals.

"If you want to live a happy life, tie it to a goal, not to people or objects."

~ Albert Einstein ~

Great People

Inspiration and encouragement is critical to goal achievement. When you intentionally expose yourself to great people, it allows you to get information to receive your desired results.

Great people pour positivity into you.

Great people ignite great things within you. Their conversation is different from others.

Great people understand that everyone is unique and they value your uniqueness.

They are not judgmental, but they provide valuable advice to help you grow. They can see you are destined for greatness and will connect you with people who can help you. You want to connect with people who have accomplished things you are going after to share guidance.

There are great people who are ready to invest in you. However, you must find them and begin to build meaningful relationships. Get around some great people.

"We need to hang around people that pour water on the fires of our fears, and throw gasoline on the passions of our dreams."

~ Kris Vallotton ~

Mentors vs. Sponsors

As women, we need more sponsors in our lives. Per a 2008 Catalyst survey, 21% of women had more than one mentor compared to 15% of men.

You may ask, why the huge gap? Men tend to have more sponsors than mentors. According to a Harvard Business Research Article, *Why Men Still Get More Promotions Than Women,* women are lacking sponsorship.

A sponsor is someone who advocates for you in and out of the room. They are in positional power and can make things happen for you. Sponsors get people promoted based on relationship currency. Do you have any sponsors?

Women are natural mentors to each other, which can overcompensate for the mentors we have in our lives.

Raise your hand if you have more than two mentors. Exactly. Now raise your hand if you have more than two sponsors.

I felt like not all hands went up on this statement. I am not saying kick your mentors to the side. I am encouraging you to put yourself out there to attract more sponsors.

You do not need permission to change. However, it would be good to know you have people talking about you positively when you are not in the room. I believe we can overcome being over mentored and under sponsored, but we must know what we want.

Think about these two questions. Do you know what you want from a sponsor? What do you want them to say about you?

Below is a chart that outlines the difference between a mentor and a sponsor.

Mentors = Advisors	Sponsors = Advocates
Serves at any level in hierarchy.	Senior leader with influence.
Personal and professional advice.	Speaks well of you and expose you to other great leaders.
Coach you to problem solve effectively.	Get you to the next opportunity and/or promoted.
Listen and provide resources for you to connect with other people.	Listen and position you to win on a higher level.

Who Are My Mentors?

____

____

____

Who Are My Sponsors?

____

____

____

Success Model

It's good to have someone in your life you look up to. My success model was my second cousin, Isis. As a little girl, I would look up to her as a ray of sunshine.

Her attitude and the tenacity of her work ethic was as loud as a sunflower. I wanted to be like Isis. Isis played the clarinet, so when I was to middle school I played the clarinet.

Isis was involved in school/community activities, so I made sure to get involved as well. I'll never forget when Isis went to Florida A&M University (FAMU).

I could remember riding the highways with my Great Aunt going to see her and hanging out around college students, attending football games, and eating at tailgates parties.

I would tag along with Isis and meet her college friends as her little cousin. Little did Isis know, I was watching her every step to map out my execution plan.

If she could do it, so could I. I am grateful to finally recognize my cousin was my success model. She was the reason I knew college was achievable, getting a career was promising, and getting married was possible.

Your success model may not be a family member; it could be someone that does not even know you exist. They may never know you are watching, so you should tell them.

I don't think my cousin truly knew she made a difference in my life. My husband persuaded me to tell her because of all the similarities he saw in us.

I told him I had learned a lot from Isis and he told me to tell her everything I had been telling him. I told my cousin in June 2016 at my Great Aunt's birthday party and I don't think I ever felt such a great embrace from her in my whole life.

Sometimes in life you must share gratitude with those who you are watching. Allow them to know how much good they put into the world and how they are making a difference in your life. Who do you look up to? Who has the level of success that you seek? I dare you to tell them that they make a difference in your life.

Haters Going To Hate

Jesus had haters, so will you. You are not exempt from haters, so get over it. My Daddy tells me all the time, *"If people are not talking about you, then you must not be doing nothing."*

Well, I must be doing a lot, sigh. The only thing you can do is handle situations better when you are around people, who are unpleasant about your personal and/or professional growth.

If you are anything like me, you stunt even more. I saw the best acronym of the word 'haters' on Instagram one day.

H – Having

A – Anger

T – Towards

E – Everyone

R – Reaching

S – Success

When you speak to people and they act like they do not want to speak back, just learn how to speak without expecting a response. A lot of people get hurt because they are expecting people to respond to their greeting.

I tell my friends all the time that sometimes you should put people in the Hey/Bye Crew. The Hey/Bye Crew consist of people who act shady and funny.

I am a Florida Girl, so it's in my blood to speak. I don't meet strangers. I love greeting people, even if they don't like me greeting them. I speak and keep it moving.

Learn how to speak and keep it moving too. Don't waste energy in trying to figure out who threw shade at you and who act like they didn't see you speaking to them.

#KeepItMoving

"Everyone is not going to love you. Most people don't even love themselves."

~ Unknown ~

Broken Relationships

You do not know how many people I meet who have given up on themselves because of what someone have said about them.

On this day, I declare that you stop allowing people that are broken, to break you. They are still broken for a reason.

It's ok if they do not give you credit. Don't allow that to diminish your character. Don't allow that to be the reason you give up on your goals. You will need to learn how to stay away from still people.

Still People Are:

Still Broke

Still Complaining

Still Hating

Still Stuck

Still Bitter

Still NOWHERE!

It could be hard to identify the 'still people' in your life. I use my discernment and often God removes people out of my life before I get the chance. Who do you need to remove out of your life?

"You don't need closure. You just need to give yourself permission to move on."

~ Steve Harvey ~

Just Say No

You should learn the art of saying no. Don't allow people to make you feel guilty when you say no.

No is a complete sentence. You need to say no without explaining yourself. It is not to offend anyone, but it is for you to defend yourself from the possibility of burnout.

I know from experience people will use you, if you let them. So, you must find power in your yes. Say yes to the people and/or things that are worthy of your time and resources. Become more aware of the things you say yes and no to.

Free of Charge

You are friends and you are cool, but you do not work for free. Real friends support your goal, your business, and your products/services financially. They should not always look for a discount.

Now, I get it. You don't want to charge them. Well, you don't have to. Just keep account of how many people you are giving products/services for free.

When I started my growth workshops in 2014, I always discounted my services or allowed some people to come from free to build my brand around my services.

After I started building my brand, there are just somethings I did not give away for free anymore.

I also kept account of how many books I gave away for free when I published my first book, *The Code to Greatness*, and it was well over 20 plus books and it was not for marketing purposes.

We (me included) should do a better job at giving away too much for free.

If people do not have the money to support you or vice versa, you can do other things like:

- Exchange products/services
- Volunteer at each other events
- Host a combined event to split costs
- Share information on social media platforms and personal email lists to help with promoting an event.

"One of the lessons that I grew up with was to always stay true to yourself and never let what somebody else says distract you from your goals."

~ Michelle Obama ~

Reintroduce Yourself

Read and complete this statement: If you know me based on who I was a year ago, you don't know me. I have grown into a Goal Getter. Let me reintroduce myself.

My name is

____

You cannot get upset with people or situations because they are powerless without your reaction. How you react to things will create your mood.

Don't allow people or situations to dictate your mood. You have the power to choose your own mood.

Choose to be happy and live in peace. Remember: Your value does not decrease based on someone's inability to see your worth.

You are worthy!

Chapter 6 Growth Journey

Summarize the main points from this chapter that will help you along your growth journey.

SELF-REFLECTION

Chapter 6 Execution List

Make a list of tasks that you need to complete to achieve your goal after reading this chapter.

TASK LIST	COMPLETION DATE
1.	
2.	
3.	
4.	
5.	
6.	
7.	
8.	
9.	
10.	

"The big secret in life is that there is no big secret. Whatever your goal, you can get there if you're willing to work."

~Oprah Winfrey ~

5TH Growth Strategy - Do Your Growth Work

Growth doesn't just happen. There must be a foundation. Let's think about how a tree grows from its roots. You plant a seed, water it, and watch it grow. Does the tree grow overnight? Do you see your oranges the next day? Nope.

I heard a great story once about the Chinese Bamboo Tree. Have you ever heard the story? After a Chinese Bamboo Tree is planted you water it just like any other plant. However, you do not see any signs of a Bamboo Tree for days, months, and even years. Would you give up?

I know my faith would be a little shaky after a year of not seeing any growth. After five years of watering the plant and the exposure to sunshine, it finally sprouts.

Wow! Not only do you see it sprout after five years, but it grows to about 80 feet in less than 6 weeks.

I love this story about the Chinese Bamboo Tree because it shows us there is no overnight process for growth. It takes time and a lot of work.

For four years that Chinese Bamboo Tree roots were strengthening itself to be able to support such a tall tree. Had the tree had weak roots, the Bamboo Tree would have fallen before anyone could see its beauty.

Are you developing and strengthen yourself for the next level? Or are you merely thinking you can achieve your goals with no work?

No Excuses, Only Growth Results

The cubicle was killing me! No matter how hard I tried to get over the thought of going to a traditional 9 to 5 Corporate America job, I couldn't shake it.

People warned me I was not fit for a desk career, but I tried it anyway. I worked in the banking industry for five years and finally said, "This is not for me." I needed to get out of this office.

I needed to be somewhere to use my talents of helping people personally grow. I used my own advice and created an exit strategy and I was out of my previous role within 6 months.

People often ask me, *"Should I leave my 9 to 5 to start my business?"* My answer is always no. I believe that you must have a strategic plan. You need an exit strategy, so do not just up and leave your job.

I used my 9 to 5 to fund my business. I worked my business during my lunch. I would read, create programs, and research during my lunch hour. I even started scheduling lunch and learns with great people.

My lunch hour became my 'start my own business' hour. What do you do on your lunch hour?

Do you really need a full hour to eat? Think about your timing needs and you can use that hour to do your growth work.

When I lost excuses, I found growth results. I no longer felt like starting my business was hard. I took it one step at a time. I no longer cared about working late at night to pursue my goals. I wrote out a list of to do items each morning to complete at night. Doing my growth work excited me to further achieve my goal.

"Excuses are a time thief. Have a goal, accept responsibility, and take action."

~Dr. Steve Maraboli ~

I saw a post on Instagram one day that blew my mind. It said, *"You can't cheat the grind. It knows how much you've invested. It won't give you nothings that you haven't worked hard for."*

Wow! The grind is real. If you not grinding, it will show in your actions. When I am working with my Goal Getter clients I am always encouraging them to keep their goal, but change the way they execute their plan.

The goal is never the problem. The problem is most likely the way in which you try to achieve your goal.

"If the plan doesn't work, change the plan but never the goal."

~ Unknown ~

Be Consistent & Stay Focused

Consistency is best friends with results. You can do anything, but not everything at one time. If you want results stay focused on one goal at a time.

See how well you do at accomplishing one goal before you move on to another one. Your consistency in daily efforts will show in the end results of goal achievement.

Stay focused on what you want, not what others want for you. Raise your hand if you feel me.

One of my Goal Getter Clients was doing so much at one time she lost sight of what she truly wanted in life.

She got money hungry and forgot about her true happiness. Don't follow opportunities, allow opportunities to follow you so you can choose the ones that best align with your goal.

Those simple money making opportunities could be distractions to your goal. Ask yourself, *"Am I consistently doing the things that will get me closer to my goal?"*

Money will come and go. Your burning desire to pursue your purpose will stay with you forever.

"Everyone must choose one of two pains: The pain of discipline or the pain of regret."

~ Jim Rohn ~

Urgency vs. Importance

Every day I prioritize my life on what's more important versus what's urgent. Sometimes the things that are of urgent may lack importance.

I time block my days by setting morning tasks, afternoon tasks, and evening tasks. If I have more tasks in either category, I decide on the tasks that must be done today because of the level of importance.

I have learned not to overwhelm myself by time blocking this way. It works. If I do not complete a task it is because it had a lower level of importance to me. You must prioritize and figure out what is important and do it first.

People like that they are busy. Child Please! The best way to accomplish your goals is to stay focused on your own __________________. (You can fill in the blank.)

Seriously, you must be committed to what you want in life. I had to release the 'busy body spirit' because it was not helping me. It was hindering me from being effective. You are not that effective when you are doing everything. Pick one thing and stay focused until you have received your desired results.

Release and Receive

There comes a time in life where we just need to release somethings. We need to release them so we can receive what God has destined for us. Below is a chart that talks about the top items I had to release, over the years, to be ready to receive all that was for me.

Release this...	Receive this...
Negative Thoughts	Daily positive affirmations, audio messages, and reading of inspirational items (i.e. The Bible, YouTube Videos, etc.) can help re-train your mindset into a positive one. Take on day at a time.
Jealously	Only compare yourself with who you were yesterday. Be grateful for your journey because it could have been worse.
Masks	You are who you are. Embrace your identity and love who you are. Remove the mask and be authentically you.
Busy Body	Slow down and be more effective in everything that you do. Busyness can make you prone to have health issues in the future.
Perfectionist	Nothing will be perfect when you start, but things can be perfected once you make mistakes. Don't be afraid of making a mistake. You can learn from them.
Victim	Stand up for yourself. You are not a victim, you are victorious in Christ Jesus.
Procrastinator	Timeliness is Godliness. Don't put off for tomorrow what you can do today.

When your mind is clouded with negative thoughts it's hard to see the positivity in life. When you are jealous of others, you lack gratitude for your life.

When you hide behind masks, you diminish your identity and could never truly create a brand story of authenticity.

When you are a busy body, you are trying to prove a point to people who don't really care about the wear and tear on your body. When you are a perfectionist, you can never appreciate the value of your work.

If your work will never be good enough for you, how can others respect it?

I struggled with producing content people would love versus what people could feel and resonate with. I am a strategist at heart, so I always want to be able to provide key strategies that people could walk away from.

However, at my 2nd Annual Personal Growth Series, my personal event where I talk about personal growth, I broke into tears sharing stories that connected to what people could feel.

I normally don't cry in public. Although, in sharing an authentic story about how my daily growth efforts allowed me to be where I am today touched my soul and could touch the soul of others.

What story do you have to share about the growth work you are doing along your journey?

Chapter 7 Growth Journey

Summarize the main points from this chapter that will help you along your growth journey.

SELF REFLECTION

Chapter 7 Execution List

Make a list of tasks that you need to complete to achieve your goal after reading this chapter.

TASK LIST	COMPLETION DATE
1.	
2.	
3.	
4.	
5.	
6.	
7.	
8.	
9.	
10.	

"I love the person I've become because I fought to become her."

~ Kaci Diane ~

6TH Growth Strategy - Reward & Praise

I love rewards, don't you? Rewards are given to someone in recognition of their service, effort, or achievement. Whenever I shop if they do not ask me to sign up for their rewards program, I always ask them if they have one.

Rewards keep me coming back, especially if it is a store that I love. Can you image giving yourselves rewards for your very own accomplishments?

Every accomplishment deserves an applause from you, first. You do not have to wait until you achieve the end goal, celebrate every little success.

You deserve to reward yourself for every small win along your growth journey. That's right, you deserve it. Remember when you were in elementary school and you passed your spelling test you would get a "Gold Star" by the teacher. Well, you are the teacher and the student in this case.

Reward yourself with something small and gradually lead up to something big in the end. I love to reward myself for the small things. One of my favorite rewards is busing a red velvet cupcake from a place called The Cup in St. Louis.

They have the best cupcakes. The place is not close to my house, so it's always a joy ride to travel and get a cupcake when I deserve it.

I also reward myself with a new pair of shoes.

I have my own shoe wall and purchasing shoes is not only a hobby put indeed a pleasure for me. I do not do these rewards at once. I choose which reward I want at the time of goal achievement.

If you

- Completed 2 job applications,
- Had an interview,
- Worked out this week,
- Wrote 10 pages in your book,
- Did some research to start your business, etc.

buy yourself something that you enjoy.

Your reward could be a nice dinner, a staycation, a massage, a new subscription, etc. or just some time to relax. After you achieve your goal you can give yourself a weekend vacation, a launch party, an "I got a new job" dinner (lol).

Whatever your goal, you deserve to reward yourself. I have never seen a track star win a race and not receive a reward at the end of the race. You deserve a trophy.

"It's not about the goal. It's about becoming the type of person that can accomplish the goal."

~ Tony Robbins ~

The Journey

You did not just go through this for a check mark. You went through this to experience the journey. You grew into this. That's why enjoying the journey is so vital.

Every obstacle you will face will only make you stronger. You are a survivor and your journey should not be overlooked once you accomplish your goal.

Embrace who you have become because the next question will be, what's next?

Your journey does not end when you accomplish your goal. It has just begun. Be ready to continually keep the cycle of goal achievement going and start a list of rewards you want in life.

Allow your reward list to be your motivation to look towards to accomplishing more goals.

Chapter 8 Growth Journey

Summarize the main points from this chapter that will help you along your growth journey.

SELF REFLECTION

Chapter 8 Execution List

Make a list of tasks that you need to complete to achieve your goal after reading this chapter.

TASK LIST	COMPLETION DATE
1.	
2.	
3.	
4.	
5.	
6.	
7.	
8.	
9.	
10.	

"When you want something bad enough you will make a way. When you don't,

you will make excuses."

~ John Rohn ~

It's Growth Time!

I believe that you can move forward once you have mastered my model of the 6 Personal Growth Strategies That Work.

1) **Divine Intervention:** You Must Seek a Higher Power to Find Your Purpose

2) **Write It Down:** You Have To See Your Goals Daily

3) **Research, and Research Again:** You Must Follow Systems That Work

4) **Build Relationships:** You Have To Develop Great Relationships

5) **Do Your Growth Work:** You Must Execute Your Personal Growth Plan

6) **Reward & Praise:** You Have To Acknowledge Your Greatness and Give Praise Where It's Due

Simply say YES to what you are called to do to make a change in this world. It is time to smile through the tears, the pain, and combat your fears.

You shall rise and move forward to achieve your goals. You cannot afford to stay stagnant when you begin to taste the freedom from being in career hostility.

You cannot afford to stay stagnant when you have seen what it is like to have inner peace with daily affirmations of positivity.

You cannot afford to stay stagnant once you have started to research what it takes to start your business. Have you ever thought about who is waiting on your gift that you are hiding from?

I remember my very first publicly known speech, *I Won't Give Up*. I was running for Miss Memorial Middle School 2002 in Orlando, Florida.

I was nervous and afraid I would mess up my speech. I rehearsed my speech a thousand times in the mirror and even said it a couple of times to my Mom and sister.

I was stepping out on stage for the first time and reciting my speech from memory. When I got on the stage (the basketball court in our gym), I held the microphone in my hand trembling and when I spoke my voice was raspy.

Before I knew it, my speech was over and people were clapping and the mic was on the floor. What in the hell!

I spoke with so much power that I threw the mic down to have an uncanny finish to my speech. When I won the title of Miss. Memorial 2002, I just knew it was an answered prayer.

I spoke in front of hundreds of people with positive words I had written.

Who knew so many people would come up to me afterwards and say that my words touched their lives. I was only a 14-year-old girl speaking from her heart. I was only sharing my gifts with the world.

You Have The Power

Imagine if you were to awaken tomorrow and your life was back on track to achieving all that you want out of life.

What if I told you, you could make that happen with simply saying: Good bye Survival, hello Thrive!

If you change the way you think about yourself, it could make a world of difference in your life. The internal battle you are fighting is much stronger than any amount of money a career can give you.

You have to start believing in yourself. If you do not believe in yourself, no one else will.

Over the years, I have found myself deeply rooted in personal growth. I am fascinated by the way I grow overtime, and I decided to study the way others grow overtime as well.

What I found is no one has to be the same person they were yesterday. You have the right to change. You have total control over who you want to be in the world. You have the power to reinvent yourself daily.

6 Things to Let Go Of Now

- Negative self-talk
- Perfection
- Fear of failure
- People pleasing
- Procrastination
- Fear of success

These 6 things will slow you down along your path of goal achievement. Sometimes these 6 things will even stop you from achieving your goals.

You must be ready to keep up the momentum despite experiencing these stumbling blocks. Notice I did not say you must be ready to move fast and forget that these things exist.

I said you simply must keep moving every day at your own pace, staying in your own lane. You can't cause an accident when you stay in your own lane.

Accidents occur when people are moving too fast, switching lanes, falling asleep at the wheel, testing while driving, not paying attention, etc.

Don't cause an accident along your journey. Stay the course and trust the process.

"When I accept myself, I am freed from the burden of needing you to accept me."

~ Dr. Steve Maraboli ~

Personal Growth Is Simple

Personal growth is simple. You either want it, unsure about it, or you are not ready to grow. You must stop trying and just do what you need to do to achieve your goals. Intentionally start working to get some results and get them accomplished on your own terms.

I Want It	I'm Unsure	I'm Not Ready
• #LetsGrow	• Keep Praying for Clarity	• What's Holding You Back?

If you are not ready to grow, then you must figure out what are your limiting beliefs?

Some Limiting Beliefs May Be:

I cannot be myself unapologetically because people may judge me.
I can't go after what I want in life because others will reject me.
It's too late to pursue my dreams and I don't want to go back to school.
No one will listen to my startup business idea.
No one will believe that I can change the world with my invention.
I can't pursue my goals because I may fail.
I need this job to pay my bills and take care of my family.
My goals can wait.

These are just some limiting beliefs I have faced or my Goal Getter Clients have faced. I am sure you have your own limiting beliefs. The only thing I can tell you is that I had to grow up and say no to the limits I had for myself from achieving my goals. I had to go back to the mirror.

You too can grow up and take action to get out of your own way to achieve your goals. I do not blame others, I simply blame myself for giving other people power over my life. I had to reclaim my power and so can you.

The 'Grow Up' Rules

- Forgive others and make peace with your past.
- Stop overthinking and take action.
- Don't compare or compete with others.
- Don't make assumptions, ask questions.
- Be willing to learn from every mistake.
- Work for what you want because no one is going to give it to you.
- Help people without wanting anything in return.
- How you start does not predict how you will finish.
- Playing the blame game is lame.
- Growth requires sacrifice, so be willing to give up something to get something greater.

Only time will tell if you are serious about growing to the next level in your life. How much time are you willing to give yourself to wake up and grow intentionally?

Be a Goal Getter

A Goal Getter breathes positivity. They are always willing to go beyond the finish line. Goal Getters can trip over stumbling blocks and thank God that they are still alive.

They embrace their journey because they know they have learned what it truly takes to intentionally achieve their goals. Are you a Goal Getter?

You have what it takes, but it will take everything to transform into a Goal Getter.

Yes, that means you will sacrifice time, money, resources, and other things you may have to achieve your goals. Sometimes life is about risking everything for a dream no one can see but you.

Are you ready to be risky? Goal Getters want it more than anything because they know if they died today, with their purpose still inside of them, they would not be leaving a legacy for their families. How bad do you want it?

6 Habits of Highly Effective Goal Getters

1. They invest in themselves.
2. They cultivate relationships.
3. They strategically execute their growth plan.
4. They add value to other people.
5. They work every day on their goal (weekends and holidays included).
6. They are unapologetic.

By applying these 6 habits you can become a highly effective Goal Getter. When things start happening for you, you will start believing. The key thing is that you must start for your plan to come true.

"Without self-discipline, success is impossible, period."

~ Lou Holtz ~

What's Next?

Now that you have all this knowledge, what are you going to do with it? Are you ready to make changes? There is no growth without change. Change can be painful, but change can also be enjoyable. It just depends on how you look at it.

I appreciate the changes in my life. I often think they are turning points in my life to make me a better person.

What I don't want to happen is you look up a year from now wishing you would have started today.

If all your life you have been paralyzed by fear of your ultimate success, then it's time for you to be restored. It's time for you to grow now. Things are happening all around us and things can change in a blink of an eye. Don't keep your greatness in a box. Let it out and share it with the world.

If you wait until you think it's the perfect time, you will be waiting for the rest of your life. There will never be a perfect time for you to start doing the things you need to achieve your goals.

That's why you must start now and do it afraid. I submitted job applications afraid, but I believed I could get a better career opportunity and I did. Being afraid doesn't mean you don't believe. Being afraid means you are not bold enough to do something. I want you to be bold enough to do whatever it takes to make your dreams come true. I want you to persist in your dream and don't give up.

"If it excites you and scares you at the same time, it might be a good thing to try."

~ Unknown~

I am a *'Confident Queen'* because I can admit the mistakes I made, the things I've learned making them, and even love myself despite my shortcomings. I have learned how to get out of my own way. Self-sabotage is real and just like I trained my mind to a more positive thinking, you can too.

I reclaimed my power, you can too. I left a career that was not fulfilling, you can too. No one is you, and that is your power. Be you and the world will adjust.

"Be careful who you pretend to be. You might forget who you are."

~ Unknown ~

An affirmation I thought you would like to read. If you need encouragement to get out of your own way and achieve your goals, read this daily.

Start now.

Start where you are.

Start with fear.

Start with pain.

Start with doubt.

Start with hands shaking.

Start with voice trembling, but start.

Start and don't stop.

Start where you are with what you have.

Just... Start.

~ Ijeoma Umebinyuo ~

Chapter 9 Growth Journey

Summarize the main points from this chapter that will help you along your growth journey.

SELF REFLECTION

Chapter 9 Execution List

Make a list of tasks that you need to complete to achieve your goal after reading this chapter.

TASK LIST	COMPLETION DATE
1.	
2.	
3.	
4.	
5.	
6.	
7.	
8.	
9.	
10.	

"Each person's task in life is to become an increasingly better person."

~ Leo Tolstoy ~

Bonus Chapter

The Goal Getters Mastermind Stories 2016

In this bonus chapter, you will get to read the stories of my first graduating class of Goal Getters here in St. Louis, Missouri.

Their stories are authentic and each one of these ladies used my CODE goal setting strategy, noted in my previous book *The Code to Greatness,* to help them achieve their personal goals. The CODE is Clarity, Options, Discipline, and Execution.

Each Goal Getter will share the good, bad, and ugly about their growth journeys. Some ladies struggled more than others. Some achieved their goals, while others didn't because of either self-discipline, self-sabotage, or even health issues.

They learned what it truly means to be a Goal Getter, which starts **internally**. They were shocked at how much growth work it required of them to craft their WHY statements before focusing on their immediate goal.

Knowing your WHY, seeing your WHY, and believing in your WHY is powerful. Your WHY keeps you focused on achieving your goal.

It propels you to keep moving whenever you have thoughts of giving up.

Some of my Goal Getters thought their WHY was one thing, but later changed it to fit their true purpose rather than pleasing other people.

Some of my Goal Getters presented me with numerous excuses in why they were not getting their growth work done. I presented them with a lot of honest feedback that disrupted the atmosphere.

Look, as a Goal Achievement Coach I believe in the client-centered approach and my clients must be able to self-reflect and point fingers at themselves before they fault anyone else. You must believe in yourself and be self-disciplined to achieve your personal goals. No excuses.

Most of my Goal Getters learned they were the reason they have not accomplished their goals. They were either complacent with where they were, hid behind other people, they rather fight the system, or they were afraid to start.

Often as women, we hide behind our insecurities and create limiting beliefs that are not actually true. Since we believe these things to be true, we create realness to unreal things. We must learn how to fight our fears with faith. We must learn how to get out of our own way.

Allow their stories to bless your soul and help you get up and get moving. Allow their stories to connect with you where you are. Allow their stories to encourage you that you can do more and you must do more if you want to achieve your goals. Remember, you hold your personal power to achieve your goals.

#ItsGrowthTime

Goal Getter Karona Wilson

My immediate goal was to write my first self-published book,

There's More In You. My WHY statement was because God said so. This is my legacy for my son and the next generation. I had to recognize there was more in ME! Also, I know I was called to help change the lives of teen Moms, single Moms, and women across the world. So, I was obedient to my assignment from God.

She opens her mouth with wisdom, and the teaching of kindness is on her tongue.

~ Proverbs 31:26~

The good thing about my journey was doing the growth work that was required of me. I learned so much more about myself. I believe in myself now, more than ever before. I can do this!

The process of self-publishing my book came with many hurdles. It seemed like every time I got to one level, something happened, and I came to a stop. This made me afraid and I was fearful to keep going.

Not fearful of my work, but fearful that this self-publishing process was too much for me. Thank God, I am a overcomer.

I now have been able to break down the wall of generational curses within my family for years. I had to face my truth and not stay where I was. I had to do something different.

Now, I can say that I am a self-published Author. Since I became an Author, I booked two speaking engagements and my books were not even printed yet. People instantly connected with my story and they saw more in me.

Along my journey, I learned so much about what I cannot tolerate. I am allergic to foolishness.

1. I'm totally necessary!

2. I'm really HARD on myself.

3. This is just the beginning of my reintroduction in my LIFE.

The advice I would give others, who would like to achieve their goal as a self-published author, is keep believing in yourself, encourage yourself, celebrate you, cry if you need to, embrace every step you take.

TIMING is important, and just because you complete your goals doesn't mean that it's the end. IT'S A JOURNEY. Life is a journey. It's ok if you don't know all the answers, but you must connect with the right people who can assist you.

You will need to stop listening to everyone's opinions of what you should do. Feed your mind with positive messages. Create affirmations and post them throughout the house.

Sow into someone else and celebrate others, but not at the expense of your peace meaning-don't pour more into someone else and you are empty.

Charm is deceitful, and beauty is vain, but a woman who fears the Lord is to be praised.

~ Proverbs 31:30~

What was your relationship like with Coach Kim during your journey?

My relationship with Coach Kim… WOW! I was bringing in the New Year on January 1, 2015 at 12:00 a.m. and I prayed that God would connect me with people who are his children with a mindset to create change. I wanted to be connected to people who could help me and I could learn from. As well as share my knowledge with them.

When I met Kim I instantly knew it was a divine connection. She has become more than my coach, she is my sister in love (friend). She is a woman with character and integrity. She has pushed me in ways I couldn't imagine. She showed me HOW and WHY. Her energy and passion to build women, as a whole, to pursue and go after their goals is contagious. She definitely has a ministry.

Coach Kim is impeccable! One day, I will open a Forbes magazine and look across the page and see her as the next Oprah Winery. I would then say to myself, "That's my coach!"

#GoalGetter2016

Goal Getter Ayesha Lindsey

My immediate goal was to create a prototype for customers who treasure their jewelry. My WHY statement was: What drives me the most is knowing that one day, I will be known to the world as an Inventress that invented thousands of products that will touch and make millions of lives better mentally, financially and spiritually.

I found great pleasure in having someone dedicated to ensure any excuse I created along the way was immediately dealt with. Excuses are mental limitations created in your mind for whatever reason and the only way to overcome them is to find the solution yourself or find someone that can guide you to the solution and that person for me was Coach Kim.

As soon as I made my decision to move full speed ahead, distractions came from every direction you can possibly think of. As bad as you may want something to work, everything happens for a reason and nothing happens without determination, discipline and drive. You must learn to push pass your obstacles and use your reason WHY to get it done. That's what Goal Getters do!

Nothing in this world is FREE, we've all heard that before. We must realize smiling and saying hello to a stranger could be your payment for something you may need later in life. Simply stating, things will get ugly, but you have to keep believing and take every opportunity when people come into your life. You never know who GOD will put in your life to lift burdens and become a resource. PICTURE it, SPEAK it, BELIEVE it, and it WILL happen!

My goal was achieved and now I consider myself to be an inventor guru. Before meeting with Coach Kim I was operating in my own bubble focusing on my own inventions.

After being challenged to do my research I know more about other inventors which has helped me tremendously in my journey. I have something the world needs and I'm doing everyone a disservice by taking so long to release it.

I learned that you have control of your destiny, no one else. Put yourself in the right circles and you'll never find yourself losing control of your destiny.

What was your relationship like with Coach Kim during your journey?

Coach Kim is a true blessing! In the next 6 months, I see myself creating a signature product for customers who treasure their jewelry. Thank you Coach Kim for your guidance and encouragement.

#GoalGetter2016

Goal Getter Adonica Radford

My immediate goal was to lose 40 pounds. A few months into the program, I reevaluated my goal to committing to living a healthier

lifestyle (daily exercising and eating healthy). My original WHY statement: I am Adonica, I am fun and love to be active, being overweight is not who I am. Then after sometime I re-evaluated my WHY statement: I am striving to be a healthier fit Adonica!

The "good" for me was accepting this challenge and taking it seriously. I was able to gain a coach and accountability partner, which helped through-out this journey. I also learned that being patient yields results. Lastly, I learned that I am an individual and what works for others may not work for me. Basically, I learned about me in the process of trying to become a new me!

The "bad" for me was several medical set-backs. I have asthma/severe allergies and diabetes. Exercising outdoors (which I prefer) led to flairs with my asthma and allergies, I was medically advised not be physically active for a few weeks. I also began a green smoothie regimen that did not yield favorable results with my diabetic condition. I had to reevaluate my food intake to get back on track to a healthy diabetic diet. It was at that time that I had to reevaluate what my goal was within this program.

The "ugly" for me was attempting to be healthy and not "see" results. When I first started this journey, I would weigh myself at least six times a day. I became addicted to weighing myself as if the number on the scale would change hourly.

When I began to see, my weight go down, I naturally became excited-until Kim challenged me to not weigh myself as much. I accepted, but failed because I was addicted to weighing myself. And, I told on myself during my check in with Kim. As a result, Kim TOOK my scale for a month!

I played like I was okay with it, and I was for the first couple of days, but around week two I was having withdrawals. It was during that time I learned how to rely on how my clothes fit and not on the number I saw on the scale.

My "ugly" became "beautiful" when I was able to put on a pair of jeans I've haven't worn for at least five years. My jeans were comfortable and I was happy.

Once Kim gave my scale back, I went straight home and weighed myself, and I dropped a couple of pounds since my last weigh in. Moral of the story, you do not have to become a slave to your scale to see a change in weight. If you eat healthy and work out, you can feel and see the results!

I released 15 pounds and considering how long I've been on my weight loss journey before the Goal Getters Mastermind Program, I think this was a great accomplishment. I often opt for instant gratification, but I've learned how to be more patient.

I've also learned to achieve my goal, with my medical conditions, I will need a team of people to assist me, such as a coach, a dietician, and a trainer.

To anyone trying to lose weight, my advice would be to stay focused and be patient. Everyone's body is different. What works for others might not work for you, and that is okay. You just have to find what works for you and that may take time. Lastly, celebrate your small milestones as huge accomplishments- you are your biggest fan and no one will celebrate you like you'd celebrate yourself.

What was your relationship like with Coach Kim during your journey?

During my journey, Coach Kim served as my indirect motivation for my goal. When I signed up for this journey I knew I needed something other than myself to motivate me. I knew since I was on her time I had to give this goal a great deal of effort. I've been on this journey off and on by myself for years and never had a good plan in place until I became a Goal Getter!

When you work with Coach Kim she makes you look deep into yourself and cut out all the excuses that are holding you back. Coach Kim, thank you for this opportunity and your dedication to me during this time. You are greatly appreciated.

#GoalGetter2016

Goal Getter Annetta Canady

My immediate goal was to move from a term employment position to a permanent position within the company I work with. My WHY statement was because I want to be an independent person and live life without limits. I have always looked out and done things for other people, expecting nothing in return.

It is now my time to be fearless and began to walk with confidence to receive a permanent positon. I believe: *"I can do all things through Christ which strengthens me."* (Philippians 4:13)

The good thing about my journey is that I took the challenges and hardships of my childhood and turned it into motivation to be something better. I was motivated, but could not figure out why other people would get the job and not me. There was a time in my life I was extremely motivated, but could not get noticed in the workplace to save my life.

The promotion of transitioning into a permanent position was happening to people all around me. It was extremely frustrating. What was wrong with me?

Coach Kim provided her expertise from being a former Customer Service Manager at prominent bank in the St. Louis area where she was a part of the hiring process.

She taught me what employers are looking for when they hire future employees and encouraged me to learn my company's culture. I got my resume updated, went to interviewing workshops at my school, explored other companies for opportunities, and went on some internal interviews.

However, there were some unforeseen internal factors on my job that prevented me from obtaining my goal of receiving a permanent position.

I found that my company's culture was hiring the most loyal person for a permanent position, not the most qualified.

I'll admit I was not as discipline as I could have been along my journey after understanding my company culture, but I was upset. I could have devoted more time each day in my job search outside the company. While I did not get a permanent position, I did lose 12 pounds during this program.

I even completed my Bachelor's degree at the University of Missouri-St. Louis in Public Policy & Administration, with a Minor in Liberal Arts. Additionally, I received certificates in Non-Profit Management and Gender Studies Women's Leadership. In the future I will leverage my degree to get me a career I am passionate about.

I learned that this may not have been the time for me to seek a permanent position within my company. I had an immediate health concern that could have prevented me from some other opportunities. Kim coached me to map out my strengths and areas for improvement. I now have an action plan to improve my job searching skills inside and outside of my current company with an intent to get a career where people will recognize my education, knowledge, skills, and expertise.

To anyone who is trying to move up in their company, but has had difficulties with their Managers and/or Human Resource Department, here is the three lessons I learned.

Lesson 1 – Don't Talk Bad About the Manager and/or Company. Talking to other coworkers about your manager and/or company creates distrust within the company. It divides the team and will always get back to the manager. Whatever disagreement you may have with the manager and/or company, go to them and talk privately about how you feel and provide solutions to problems.

Lesson 2 – Effort Is Noble. Failure may happen, but never plan for it, never accept it, and never ever assume you will fail. Have a winning attitude. Do what it takes, and leverage the strengths to surround yourself with people who can mentor you in your role to get you to the next level. Make the effort to get your career to the next level.

Lesson 3 – Own Everything, Wins and Losses. The minute I started making excuses is the minute I start avoiding my own actions. If you mess up, take ownership for it. This will make you an accountable and responsible person. Admit it was your fault. Here's why, things went wrong and you can finally figure out what you will do differently to prevent a situation from happening again.

What was your relationship like with Coach Kim during your journey?

Kim, I would like to personally thank you for investing your time into me. Thanks for having the vision to want to help others to achieve. Our relationship was a two-way communication.

As a coach, you were expanding your communication and leadership skills. I was gaining a personal sense of satisfaction from knowing that I had someone expand my viewpoints, and consider new ways of approaching situations. I felt we both improved our communication skills, learn new ways of thinking, and ultimately how to advance in our careers.

As a coach, you supported me by asking tough questions, encouraging me to take action, and expressed how I should move toward my goal by mapping out my career path. Thank you.

#GoalGetter2016

Goal Getter Amber Gatkins

My immediate goal was to lose 30 pounds during the program. I decided to take this journey because I was not comfortable in my own skin. My why was because I deserve to be a healthier me and not succumb to my fear of being a diabetic like many of the members of my family.

Throughout this journey, I have learned to be comfortable in my own skin. I know losing weight is not something that's not going to happen overnight, so I embraced loving me, which is absolutely essential.

Coach Kim has given me tools to not only accomplish this goal, but many other goals in the future. I also found out so much about myself that I did not know and probably would not have known if it wasn't for connecting with other women in the Goal Getters Mastermind Program.

The 'bad' for me during this process was that I would beat myself up when I would get off track. Life happens.

Some days I would eat great and work out, while on other days my work schedule would change and mess up my schedule. This frustrated me many times and I would sulk in frustration instead of looking at tomorrow as a new start.

The 'ugly' was coming to the realization that I lack self-discipline. I do not know how to tell myself no and I think that was my biggest downfall. I love pizza and I would tell myself, "Of course you can have it, It's Friday."

However, I paid for it and this stifled my weight loss process. I only loss 15 pounds. Had I been able to say no to myself my results would have been different. I still celebrated know how much work it took me to lose weight and how much work Coach Kim put into teaching me to write out the key steps I needed to let go to achieve my goal.

I initially felt getting my finances in a stable place was my primary goal but I decided later my health was more important. Throughout the process of working on my primary goal, I applied Coach Kim's processes and teachings and I was able to manage my finances. I feel more financially responsible.

First and foremost, I learned that if I do my growth work, I can accomplish any of my goals. I had a pessimistic view of myself. So, I had to learn how to love me first and my mindset is changing. Learning that I lacked self-discipline was probably the biggest ah-ha moment for me during this program. I will continue to be self-reflective in my actions. Lastly, I learned that traditional working out does and meal prepping does not work for me. I prefer going to boot camp and possibly having someone else prep my meals.

To anyone trying to lose weight, celebrate the small accomplishments and use them to push you further. Remember that tomorrow is a new day and if it has to be "Day 1" again, make it a better "Day 1". Find out what works best for you. You do not have to follow traditional steps. Research and try different processes and then decide on what you will go with. It's your journey, no one else, so embrace it and roll with the punches.

What was your relationship like with Coach Kim during your journey?

Coach Kim was absolutely AMAZING! I truly needed someone to push me and hold me accountable and she did that and much more. Kim called, texted, and emailed me on a regular basis.

She held me accountable with simple texts asking me what I ate. Many times, she made me feel convicted of my actions, and I truly needed that tough love. I loved that Kim believed in me when I did not believe in myself. She saw the beauty in me that failed to see at times. I felt Kim was genuine and really understood my good, bad, and ugly days.

Many people struggle in finding what their purpose in life, but I truly believe Kim is not one those people. She has been such a blessing in my life. I am beyond grateful and pray that in her pursuit to help others she will receive all the success she dreams of because she deserves it. Thank You Kim!

#GoalGetter2016

Goal Getter Alexis Brewer

My immediate goal was to lose 25 pounds by July 1, 2016. I chose this as my goal because I felt like I had tried many different weight loss methods, yet could not reach and maintain my goal. I felt that partnering with Kim would be a great way for me to get a boost of motivation and confidence to start achieving my goal.

Kim did an excellent job of pushing me outside of my comfort zone and helping me to remember why I started in the first place. My WHY Statement was I wanted to lose 25 pounds because I wanted to be a healthier me, love the way I feel in my clothes, and love the way I look when I saw myself in the mirror to have a lasting confidence within myself.

The good thing about my experience is that I was able to make healthier eating choices and make more of a conscious effort to make better decisions on the foods I was using to nourish my body. I learned more about portion control, how to meal prep, and how fun activities can count as exercise. Kim really taught me the importance of consistency.

The bad part of my experience was my tendency to get lazy. I did not want to spend the time cooking or prepping meals in advance, and I did not financially have the funds to pay someone to prep my meals for me. So, I let my choices on what I ate and the life circumstances that I endured during this time dictate how well or poorly my day went.

I was really starting to face reality and I found out what happens when I choose to veer off from my steps in achieving my goal. I had to realize that there was no magic formula. I had to simply do the required growth work, be consistent with my eating habits and work out plan, and believe that the results would come.

I got in my own way of achieving my weight loss goal, but I did see inches disappear at my waist line. I saw a difference in how my clothes fit and it boosted my self-confidence. I've learned so much about myself and now I realize that this journey was not so much about losing weight at all.

My journey was about loving Alexis. I learned that I do have the power within me to achieve anything if I put my mind to it. I have also learned what it truly means to become fearless and intentional about reaching any goals I will set for the future. Fear has no part in my success.

The advice that I would like to give to others who want to live a healthier lifestyle is to always remember why you want to do this. Keep your WHY Statement somewhere where you can see it and recite it every day. Go even further to memorize it as you would your favorite quote or song.

Remembering your why statement will help keep you in line with your goal and will keep you from losing focus. Understand that if your goal is to live a healthier lifestyle it takes time, consistency, and lots of work. Practice self-care and love yourself no matter what size you are. Don't put so much pressure on yourself. Realize that small changes lead to big results.

What was your relationship like with Coach Kim during your journey?

My relationship with Coach Kim was very warm and nurturing during this experience. I consider myself to be very shy and quiet, yet Kim still found a way to get me to open up and share my deepest thoughts and feelings with her. I loved that she gave so much of herself during this time and allowed us to reach out to her at any time (even for small things). I recall one time reaching out to her because I was going out to lunch with a friend. She was very helpful in giving me restaurant suggestions that had healthy menu items.

Kim taught me the importance of being consistent and I will continue to use her methods to achieve future goals. I am not a very detail-oriented person, so to see how Kim was able to break down my goal into smaller steps, and show me how those small steps lead to an even bigger picture was truly amazing.

Kim is like that sister or girlfriend that you want and must have in your inner circle. She's very up front and honest, but I knew she genuinely cared about me and my success. When I struggled with achieving my goal, she helped me to take my own journey of self-love and acceptance. I had a great experience through this entire journey and I recommend Kim to anyone needing that extra boost in reaching any goal, no matter how big or small.

#GoalGetter2016

When I read their stories, I got teary eyed. I worked with these women and saw firsthand what they went through along their growth journeys. It's always good to have great people who believe in you. I love these women and I enjoyed being their Goal Achievement Coach who not only pushed them to achieve their goals, but gave them growth strategies they can use forever.

If you want to join the Goal Getter Movement and be a part of my next Goal Getters Mastermind Program then go to www.coachkimburke.com to learn more. I would love to be your coach along your growth journey.

Chapter 10 Growth Journey

Summarize the main points from this chapter that will help you along your growth journey.

SELF REFLECTION

Chapter 10 Execution List

Make a list of tasks that you need to complete to achieve your goal after reading this chapter.

TASK LIST	COMPLETION DATE
1.	
2.	
3.	
4.	
5.	
6.	
7.	
8.	
9.	
10.	

ABOUT THE AUTHOR

Kimberly Burke is considered the epitome of what you can achieve if you set goals and work hard to accomplish them. She is an unapologetic Goal Getter. Her philosophy is simple: *"If people want to achieve their goals, then they will achieve their goals."* She started her professional coaching company, Queen Kim Enterprises, LLC to equip and inspire people to achieve their goals.

As a Goal Achievement Coach, she helps transform Goal Setters into Goal Getters with her realistic experiences, cutting edge growth strategies, innovative tools and comprehensive execution plans. As a result of young professional women working with Coach Kim, they gain more clarity about the goals they want to achieve right now. They learn why maintaining a high level of self-confidence and eliminating negative self-talk is the key to their personal greatness. She focuses on getting them past stop signs in their lives with execution plans that can be used immediately.

Kimberly studied Psychology at Florida A&M University and graduated magna cum laude with a Bachelor of Science degree. She studied Management and Leadership at Webster University in St. Louis, where she graduated with honors and earned a Master's degree. She is a Certified Coach, Teacher, Trainer, and Speaker with The John Maxwell Team.

Kimberly has been featured in local and national newspapers, magazines, and television related to her expertise in goal achievement. As a bestselling author and an award-winning speaker, Coach Kim empowers people to move from stagnation to results.

Find out more details at www.coachkimburke.com to view articles, watch interviews, and view upcoming events that the author may have.

She is married to Al Thomas and resides in Saint Louis, Missouri.

Contact Kimberly Burke

Do you want Coach Kim to be the next Guest Speaker at your event? Do you need a life coach who can help you execute like a Goal Getter? Contact her today to tell her about your event and/or goal you are trying to reach.

#ItsGrowthTime

Email: info@coachkimburke.com

Website: www.coachkimburke.com

Follow the Author on Social Media @CoachKimBurke

BOOKS BY KIMBERLY BURKE

The Code to Greatness Book

The Code to Greatness: A Goal Setting Cycle That Will Help You Achieve Any Goal (2014). Everyone has dreams they would like to see come true, but they will not become a reality until you do your growth work. So, what's the CODE? The CODE is a simple four phase cycle that is an acronym for Clarity, Options, Discipline, and Execution.

Each phase pushes people to live out their best possible self by doing their growth work and encourages them that they are enough to make their dreams a reality. The Code to Greatness is a MUST read for students, young professionals, and anyone who is going through life transitions and need to find clarity about their life goals. The CODE is a simple strategy that you can implement immediately.

Purchase today www.coachkimburke.com**.**

Also sold on Amazon and Amazon Kindle.

The 28 Day Growth Challenge

Replace fear with confidence, set clear goals, and achieve them with Coach Kim's 28 Day Growth Challenge.

You will receive one module that encompass 28 questions that will get you clear, motivated, and ready to take action. With this challenge, you will

1) Discover your WHY,

2) Create new goals,

3) Eliminate negative self-talk,

4) Get out of your own way.

28 days is enough time for you to

1) Put yourself first,

2) Be intentional,

3) Plan your work, and work your plan,

4) Achieve your goals.

Purchase your copy today www.coachkimburke.com**.**

20 Beautiful Women: Volume 4: 20 More Stories That Will Heal Your Soul, Ignite Your Passion, And Inspire Your Divine Purpose

"20 Beautiful Women: 20 More Stories That Will Heal Your Soul, Ignite Your Passion And Inspire Your Divine Purpose" is a collection of personal short stories from 20 more authors, speakers, and life coaches bonding together for the common goal of sisterhood, and to transform women from the inside out."

Many of these stories, told here for the very first time, will empower you to make real changes in your life, heal down to your soul, find your passion, and live your divine purpose, now. This compelling book is a must read for anyone desiring connection with other real women and true transformation.

My personal story is Chapter 13: My C.O.D.E to Greatness. In this chapter I share my personal story of abandonment at the age of 16. I provide you with the strategy I used to find my personal greatness despite my growing pains. You will also learn how I became a Goal Getter and why I am passionate about personal growth.

Purchase your copy today www.coachkimburke.com**.**